# Symbols of Freedom

by Elizabeth West

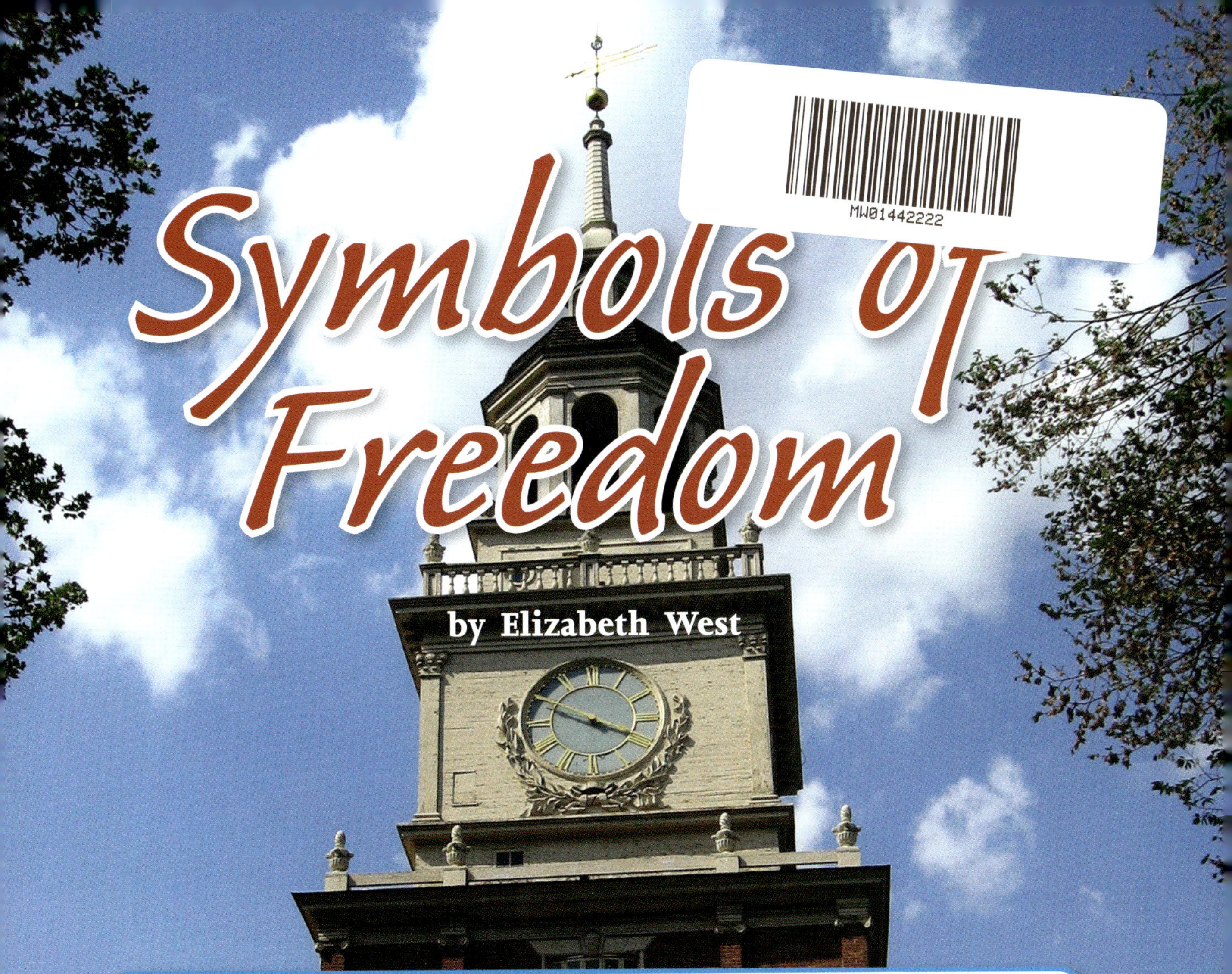

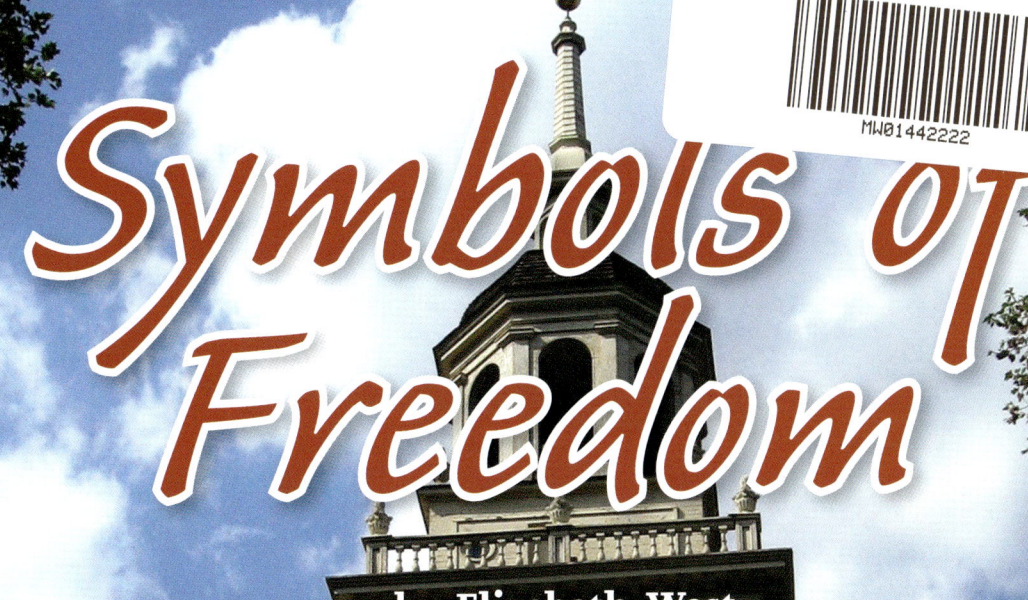

## Table of Contents

| | |
|---|---|
| Get Started | inside front cover |
| Symbols of Our Nation | 2 |
| The Declaration of Independence | 3 |
| The American Flag | 4 |
| The Liberty Bell | 6 |
| Respond and Go Beyond | 8 |
|     Stretch Your Brain | 8 |
|     Read a Map | inside back cover |

# Symbols of Our Nation

The United States (U.S.) is a nation, or country.
The U.S. won **freedom** from Great Britain during the American Revolution.
The American Revolution was fought from 1771 to 1781.

Our nation has many **symbols**.
These symbols help us remember our nation's history.
They help us remember our belief in freedom.
There are three very important U.S. symbols.

**This parade in historic Williamsburg, Virginia helps us remember the American Revolution.**

# The Declaration of Independence

The Declaration of Independence is an important symbol of the United States. This **document** was written in 1776. It said that the American **colonies** were free. It said that the United States and Great Britain were separate nations. Today, this document is a symbol of our freedom.

Thomas Jefferson wrote the Declaration of Independence. He made changes as some ideas were debated.

## Connect Skills to Language

Some words give clues for finding a **main idea**. Words such as *important*, *main*, or *key* may show a main idea. Phrases such as *there are* or *there have been* may show a main idea. For example, this sentence on page 2 states a main idea:

There are three very important U.S. symbols.

Reread page 3. Which sentence states a main idea? Which sentences give **details** that support the main idea?

# The American Flag

The American flag is an important symbol of the United States. Some people call our flag "The Red, White, and Blue." Some people call our flag "The Stars and Stripes." People all over the world know our flag.

## I DIDN'T KNOW THAT!

The 13 stripes on the American flag stand for the first 13 colonies. The colors on the American flag are symbols, too. White is a symbol of innocence. Red is a symbol of courage. Blue is a symbol of fairness.

**The U.S. flag flies all day and night at the White House.**

There have been different U.S. flags in our history.
The 13 American colonies became the first 13 states.
So the first U.S. flags had 13 stars.
Each time a new state was added to our country, a star was added.
There were other changes, too.
Look closely at the flags to see how they differ.

**From 1795-1818 the U.S. flag had 15 stars and 15 stripes. Later, the flag went back to just 13 stripes.**

**Official flags with different numbers of stars hang at the U.S. Capitol. How many states were there when each flag was designed?**

## Connect Skills to Strategies

What are the **main ideas** on pages 4 and 5? Look for clues that help you **determine importance**, or find the most important ideas. Look at the headings, captions, and pictures. Look for clue words in the sentences. Find the main idea on each page. Then find some **details** that support the main ideas.

# The Liberty Bell

The Liberty Bell is an important American symbol. This bell was made in England in 1752. It was sent to the colony of Pennsylvania. The bell was hung in the State House. It was called the State House bell. **Colonists** rang the bell for meetings.

**The State House is in Philadelphia, Pennsylvania. Today it is called Independence Hall.**

## AMAZING BUT TRUE

During the American Revolution, colonists hid the bell. They did not want the British to melt it down to make a cannon!

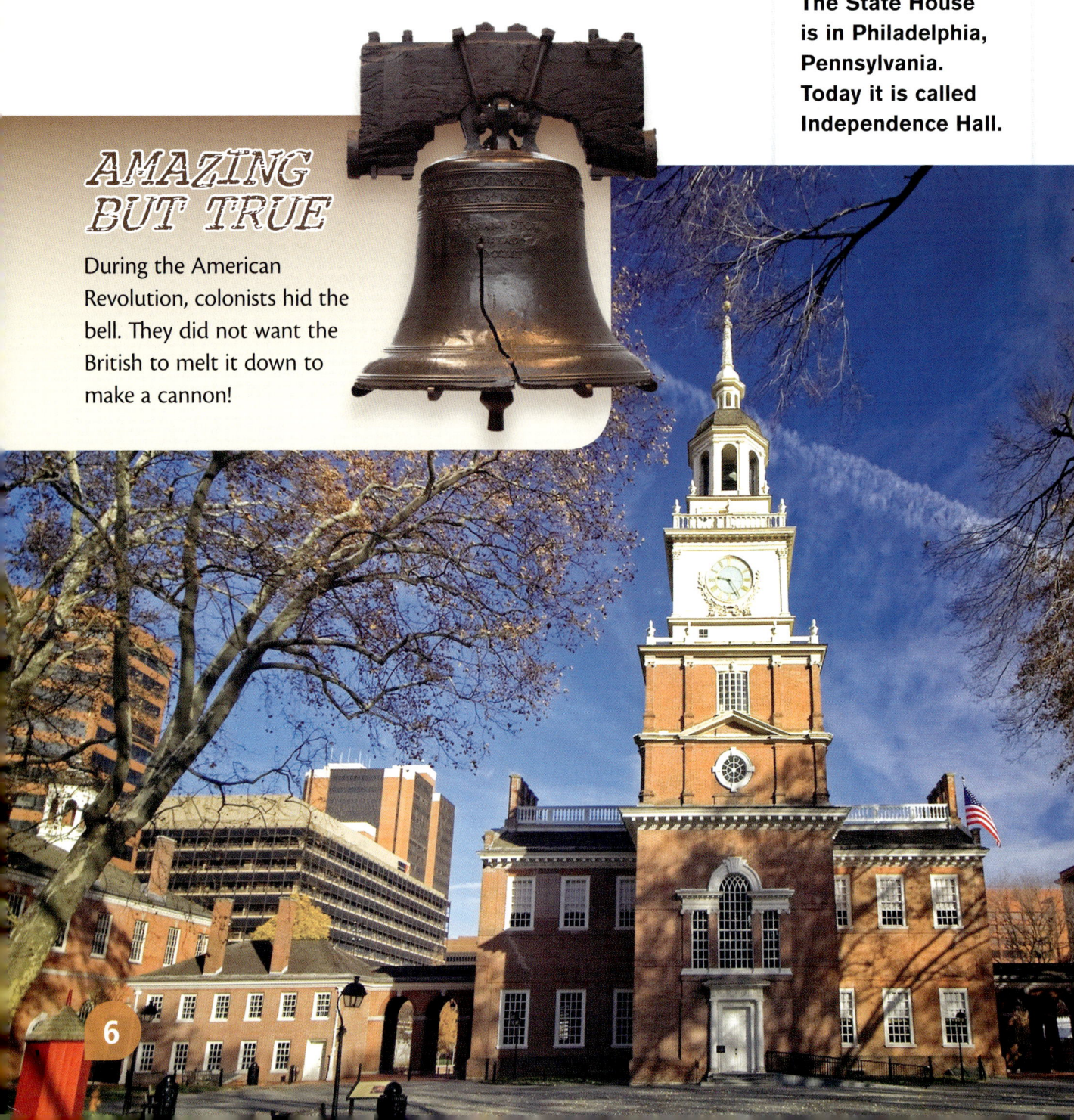

"Liberty" means freedom. Today, many people visit this symbol of our freedom.

The bell cracked the first time it was rung.
People used the metal to make a new bell.
Over time, the new bell cracked, too.
In 1846 the crack got so big that the bell could not ring.

By then, the bell had rung for many special events.
It had rung to announce battles and new laws.
It had rung to celebrate presidents.
People had started to call it the Liberty Bell.
The bell became a symbol of freedom.

### Put It All Together
The United States has important symbols.
These symbols help us remember the American Revolution.
They help us remember the importance of freedom.

## Connect Skills to Your Life

How does **identifying main idea** and **details** help you:

- learn more about the American Revolution?
- understand important symbols?
- write about your own ideas?

# Respond and Go Beyond

## Share Ideas | After Reading

What can we learn from important symbols of the United States? Share what you learned with a partner.

## Connect Skills to *Symbols of Freedom*

**Identify Main Idea and Details with a Graphic Organizer**

Create a graphic organizer like this one. Write a main idea for each symbol in this book. List details that support the main ideas. Talk about your graphic organizer with a partner.

**Use the Strategy** Look for clues that help you determine importance, or find important information. Use these clues to find the main ideas and supporting details.

**Symbols of Freedom**

| | | |
|---|---|---|
| **Main Idea:** The Declaration of Independence is an important symbol of freedom. | **Main Idea:** The American flag is ____. | **Main Idea:** The Liberty Bell is ____. |
| **Details:** It was written in 1776. It said that ____. | **Details:** | **Details:** |

### Write About It!

Write a paragraph about a symbol in this book.
- Give some details about this symbol.
- Tell why this symbol is important.

### Stretch Your Brain

**Design a postage stamp!**

Design a new postage stamp. Choose an American symbol for your design. Draw a picture of the new stamp. Explain your design to a partner.